KENT
LETTERS

Students' Responses to May 1970 Massacre

BARBARA BECKER AGTE

KENT LETTERS Students' Responses to May 1970 Massacre
by
Barbara Becker Agte

ISBN 978-0-9823766-6-9

Library of Congress Control Number: 2012930035

Book Design
Bette Waters

Cover and letter photos
Barbara Agte

Author photo
Tim McAndrews

Bluwaters Press
P. O Box 1705
Deming, NM 88030
www.bluwaterspress.com

CONTENTS

INTRODUCTION KENT LETTERS

Letters, poems, essays, and comments from my students at the time of the May 1970 tragedies began to arrive at my home and at my office on the KSU Campus in June of 1970. The letters, etc. were responses to a request for a final paper to complete the requirements for their English class.

(The KSU Administration directed all instructors to contact each student enrolled during the spring quarter and tell him or her how to complete the courses. On May 4, students as well as staff members were told to leave campus by 3 in the afternoon and return when notified.)

My letter to my students said I hoped each was well, that I was dreadfully sorry their time at Kent had been cut short, that I was shocked and horrified their friends and classmates had been killed or injured, and that the administration had asked me to contact them to give instructions for completing their class at Kent. I asked each student to please send me whatever he or she had written about the Kent tragedies. The letter's last sentence said their final grade for the class would be an A.

With each letter I included a copy of Yevgeny Yevtushenko's poem "Bullets and Flowers" which had been translated from Russian by THE NEW YORK TIMES shortly after May 4.

A few notes from students arrived soon, some later. A number of students telephoned or came to visit, saying they simply could not write about the tragedies. Wondering if I myself would have been

4

able to write anything to show an instructor, I accepted their verbal responses as a completion of the course. While I did not have the foresight to record their comments, it has been brought to my attention by a former student that several of those conversations were evidently recorded and filmed by the FBI.

In fall of 1970, unsure of what to do with the letters, I stuffed them into a large, battered, manila envelope. For years, I simply stored the collection of letters in the back of a filing cabinet drawer. In 2005, in response to a request from KSU Honors College, I typed all the letters and designed a readers' theatre presentation of them. The Honors College did not choose to accept my proposal, but now, because of world unrest, and because I do not wish the letters to be lost, I have chosen to publish them.

And so, Dear Readers, please find the written works of the students in my two classes of Freshman English in the spring of 1970 at Kent State University. With the students' works, I have included a copy of "Bullets and Flowers," by Yevtushenko and a copy of my remarks at the 25th KSU Commemoration of May 4, 1970. Lastly, I have included a listing of works I have read and reread which, from my point of view, are essential to reviewing the times and the events.

When deciding to publish the students' works, I considered first contacting students who had written to me. Since that task, although attempted, was never fully accomplished, writers are only identified by their initials, dates from their letters' postmarks, the names of the states in which the letters were posted. The letters and other works appear in no particular order; I typed them as I took them out of their envelope five years ago.

Should students chose to contact me, I would be delighted. (Rereading the letters these past months reminded me often how beautifully earnest and honest my students were and how much I enjoyed them.) Presently, I am the only Barbara Agte with a listed telephone phone in Columbus, New Mexico, U.S.A. BBA

R.M. May 29, 1970 - Ohio

Dear Mrs. Agte,

I wanted to tell you that I enjoyed taking 161 and 162 English with you. Our discussions and topics were most interesting. The outcome of the disorders, and demonstrations has affected me a great deal. I really miss Kent State, and can hardly wait for it to reopen. The shootings have really affected me and others I have talked to. I hope that our government and its leaders will have learned a lesson from their outcome.

Thanks again. R.M.

WHAT CAUSED THE DEATHS AT K.S.U.?

There are many reasons that are responsible for the deaths of four students at Kent State. The reasons are not primarily the movement of troops into Cambodia, the war in Viet Nam, the suppressions of the black students' demands, but reasons far more important exist. Reasons such as, lack of communication, lack of respect, lies, and the use of violence to condemn violence caused four young students to be slain on the K.S.U. campus.

The whole Kent disorder started from a small spark on that Friday night and exploded into a bomb which led to the killing of four innocent youths on the following Monday. The reason for the actual shootings will probably never be revealed.

And a much sadder thing is that some people

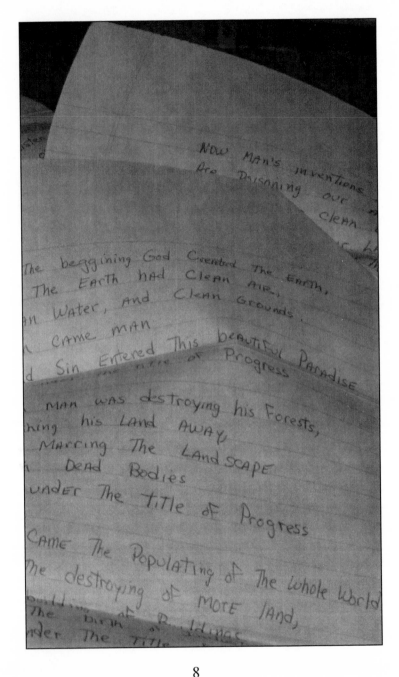

actually feel that the shootings were justified. Feelings, such as these, are what caused the students to die. People who have no respect for human life or even students' demands are what the students, on most of the college campuses, are fighting for.

How can any student have respect for the government when it sends thousands of soldiers to Viet Nam , to kill people for a very unrealistic cause?

Or, how can a student respect a police officer, or force, that beats kids, just because they have long hair or tear gasses a crowd of students because they have grouped together peacefully to protest something they strongly believe is wrong.

Another aspect which led to the slaying at Kent State is that throughout our lives, we have been told lies, and these lies, which must stop, cause us to be non-believers in those who lie to us. For example, Sunday night a rally took place on the front campus.

This rally, a peaceful one, was to last until one o'clock (the curfew on campus). But at about eleven o'clock the tear gas started pouring down, thus angering the students to no end.

There was no cause for the tear gas, except maybe because the police got tired of standing around, but they did it anyway.

The same thing happened Monday, but the result of this was the death of four students, not even taking part.

When a high official in office publically announces that he will not be concerned with what the people feel or think about his actions and calls students "bums" this is a lack of communication.

This probably is the most serious thing that is responsible for the disorder.

The most important thing that people have with one another is communication, and to show no concern for the feelings or ideas of other people is a most serious lack of responsibility. The President of the U.S. showed lack of responsibility.

The most unjustifiable thing, or action used with all of the other causes is the use of violence to condemn violence.

Every time the police tear gassed a crowd, beat someone, or used the National Guard to help enforce them, this triggered the students to disrespect them more and more until death resulted.

Incidents such as the stabbing of a girl, students rifle-butted or getting one's face slashed are totally unrealistic. But as the students of Kent State found out, these acts were nothing; the Guard would even kill people.

These actions caused the majority of the students on campuses in the United States to lose respect for the government, the police and for the people who order these organizations to become involved with the students. It also caused many other people to die or get injured for fighting for this great lack of communication and respect that exists in our society today.

The saddest thing is that the ones that were killed, really didn't know why they were the ones chosen to die.

There was no excuse for their deaths, and the fact that we have created a society in which a thing like the Kent incident can occur is frightening.

Kent State University is now a shrine, known the world over for the deaths and injuries of its students.

The real facts will probably never be told, for they are surely to disgrace our National Guard. One thing is for certain, our society is in a lot of trouble, and if something isn't done about it soon, it will undoubtedly fall like others have throughout history.

R.M.

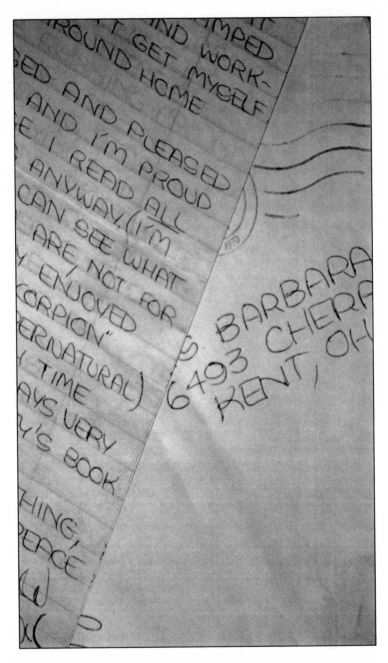

T.H. June 15, 1970 - OHIO

Barbara,

Thank you for allowing me to [stay] at your place. After being on the road for about 30 hours, it was great to sleep in a bed.

By the way, remember Paul who was traveling with you when you picked me up? Well, he was on the beach at Coronado, Calif., and he saw my pack and came up to me. Another point in favor of "it's a small world."

If you are ever in Boston, don't worry about anything just get in touch with me. My parent's address: ____.

Will write soon. Was on my way to see you, but got a ride to Iowa. Gotta hurry. See you soon. Will write.

DEATH

When you see them
tell them I am still here,
that I stand on one leg while the other one dreams,
this is the only way

that the lies I tell them are different
from the lies I tell myself,
that by being both here and beyond
I am becoming a horizon,
that as the sun rises and sets I know my place
that breath is what saves me,

that even the forced syllables of decline and death,
that if the body is a coffin it is also a closet of breath,

That breath is a mirror clouded by words,
that breath is all that survives the cry for help
as it enters the stranger's ear
and stays long after the word is gone
that breath is the beginning again, that from it
all resistance falls away, as meaning falls
away from life, or darkness falls from light,
that breath is what I give them when I send my
love.

T.H.

W.H. May 24, 1970 - OHIO

On May 4, 1970, I decided to go to the Commons for a rally scheduled at noon. I did not know what to expect, but it turned out to be a day I will never forget. My roommate, T., and I arrived shortly after 12:00. I felt that the students had something to demonstrate about, and I thought the rally was reasonably peaceful.

In my opinion only about 1% of the students there were throwing rocks and I just couldn't understand how any of the National Guardsmen were in danger of losing their lives. About 12:30 I was in a crowd that got tear-gassed, and I'm sure I will never forget it in my entire life. I had tears in my eyes, and I was dizzy. I still do not understand why we were tear-gassed, however. The students at that time were peaceful. Between 1:00-1:30 my roommate and I were on top of Taylor Hall Hill. I will never forget what happened at this time.

We were standing real close together when another tear gas canister was shot into the crowd. A student picked up the canister and threw it back at the National Guardsmen. A Guardsman picked up the canister and threw it back at us. The same student threw the canister back at the Guardsman. Then I saw about one-half Guardsmen drop to one knee. I looked toward my roommate in disbelief.

I wasn't scared at all because I thought for sure that if they would shoot that they would shoot over our heads. Then the moment occurred. It was

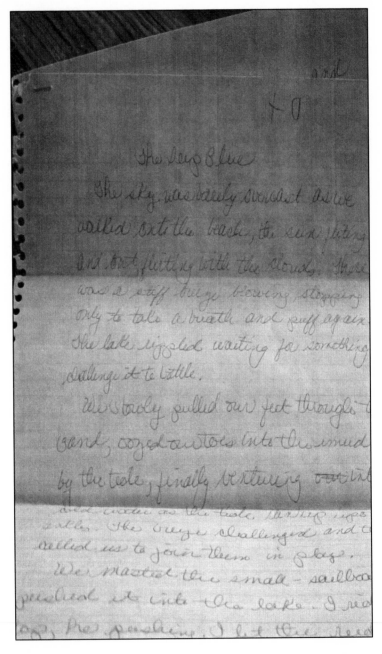

like machine gun fire. A boy ten feet from my room-mate and me was shot, and I'm sure he was dead.

My roommate and I ran. After a while we came back and regrouped. I saw at least four to five innocent students put into ambulances. I personally knew Allison Krause who was killed by bullet fire.

In my personal opinion there was not [a] sniper. If there was, I am sure that the NATIONAL Guardsmen shot first. I felt that the Guard should have made sure who they were shooting at. I feel it was murder and inexcusable for the Guardsmen to shoot.

W.H.

M.H. June 7, 1970 - OHIO

Dear Mrs. Agte,

Sorry our time at Kent was cut so short this spring. I really enjoyed being in your class.

I am now working in the payroll department for the summer at my father's plant.

Hope you have a very enjoyable summer and God willing, we may meet next fall.

Sincerely yours,

M.H.

THE KENT TRAGEDY

I firmly believe in peaceful demonstrations but when these demonstrations become violent and destructive, they lose their very purpose. Masses become uncontrollable, property is damaged, citizens become enraged, and personal health is endangered, and in the Kent State case, death was the climax.

This tragedy will be a mark on Kent State University and will be in the memories of people everywhere for years to come. Is this the way we want to get the action we are looking for?

If Kent State students had been allowed to carry on these demonstrations without the intrusion of professional agitators and radical instigators, this sad and tragic event may have never occurred.

Do we have the right to blame the National Guard? Guns should always be respected and considered at all times loaded. The students were warned time and again and after 3 full days of pleading, warning, and threatening: they disobeyed and disregarded the National Guard which is part of our civilian protective society. What can we expect?

The ultimate catastrophe is the four innocent victims and I wonder if those responsible know what they started.

M.H.

Dani
Engl
May

-1-

Governor Rhodes fault.
hen the guard came to kent
know who was responsil
eir being here. I wen't t
- University that weekend an
returned to school, all I sa
smen. I figured President
rested The National Gu
g to news

Student who rescued Tom

Barbara Becker Agte

M.B. June 1, 1970 - NEW YORK

Dear Agtes,

Thanks again for being so great to us when we were in Kent. Oberlin [Oberlin College allowed Kent Students and faculty to gather at their campus, creating Kent State University in Exile] was very interesting. I'm glad to see people getting together to improve that prison we call a University.

Life in B. is getting to be a drag. It's impossible for a "big hair" to get a job. It looks like it's going to be no hair or no money.

I hope you are having a great summer. If you [are] in B., drop by.

All power to the people.

Crush the war machine.

M.B.

KENT STATE - MAY 4, 1970

The horrors and the tragedies of the afternoon of Monday, May 4, 1970, will remain with me for the rest of my life. The senseless massacre, of harmless students, begging for their rights, by a group of bloodthirsty national Guardsmen still haunts me.

It was a beautiful May afternoon on the Kent State campus. However, the student's minds were on something far more important than the weather. The governor, obsessed with winning an election at all costs to anyone but himself, had sent 2000 Guardsmen to our campus. The students' political views had

21

KENT LETTERS Students' Responses to May 1970 Massacre

differed greatly, but at this point they all agreed on one issue. Angry voices yelled, "Get those pigs out now."

The campus was no longer a place for learning, but rather a military battlefield. It was impossible to go anywhere or even speak to anyone outside a dormitory.

At noon there was a rally scheduled on the commons. When we arrived, there were already thousands of frenzied students and faculty screaming and chanting. Across the commons, about 100 yards away, stood guardsmen in full battle dress, their trigger fingers itching and their mouths watering for blood.

A jeep pulled up and a man with a bull horn told us we were not allowed to congregate on our own campus. The students replied, "Go to hell."

Moments later a barrage of pepper gas engulfed us. This forced us back into the dorms located just above the commons. We students, angrier than ever now, ran to Prentice Hall to get the gas out of our eyes.

We emerged from the building into the parking lot. There, we saw a small unit of guardsmen on the practice football field. They tried to drive us back with more gas.

After a few minutes the guardsmen got into formation and jogged up a nearby hill, next to Taylor Hall.

The students followed them closely, using their mouths as their only weapons. As the guard-men reached the top of the hill, they turned. The ones in front dropped to one knee and those in the rear leaned over them. As if a command had been issued, they all began to fire in unison.

My first impression was that they were firing blanks to scare us; but to stay safe, I hit the dirt. After the volley of shots, which seemed to last forever, I heard the boy next to me shout, "They shot my foot off."

I was terrified. My first reaction was to look to see where the guardsmen were. They had vanished. I quickly picked up the injured student. As I turned around, I saw another student lying on the road about ten feet behind me. His head had been destroyed and blood was gushing out in thick gelatin-like globs.

I knew he was dead—but I could not believe it. I had never seen a dead person. I was sick.

I then carried the injured student to Prentice Hall. As we walked through the parking lot, there were petrified and wounded students everywhere. The area had the aura of a battlefield. I put the student on a couch in Prentice Hall. A girl began to administer first aid to him.

I WENT BACK OUT. It was like a bad trip. I could not believe that I was at Kent State. Blood and terror were everywhere. There were no doctors or ambulances. All the phone lines had been cut and there was no way of reaching help. It seemed like hours before the ambulances came and took the wounded students away.

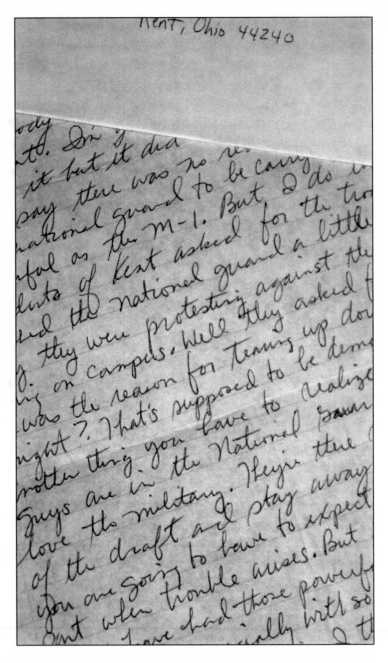

Later the bewildered students again gathered on the commons, this time in greater force and all brimming with anger. We wanted revenge! Again the man with the bullhorn appeared. This time he told us he would kill us all if it were necessary.

The angry students finally dispersed, but each will remember forever the horrors of May 4 at Kent.

M.B.

reason the real ...t hasn't let me stood
relapses & night mares.
I am tired & worn o
...ine I git up in the
9. With all this & th...
- It has caused me ...
...y & I'm afraid I...
...see a psychologist &
...e can help me out
...ough of that.
...e ted & I hear he
...writing me soon.
...t forward to it. I

J.C. June 11, 1970 - OHIO

Dear Mrs. Agte,

I am so sorry I haven't written sooner. I have been trying to write a paper about the incidents at Kent, but somehow I feel there is nothing to write. There is no way I can express my grief, every paper I write seems more trite than the one before.

In my few weeks home, I have discovered what my "wonderful" hometown is really like; and to think I was part of it!! The people here do not sympathize at all with K.S.U. I keep hearing "THOSE COMMUNIST TROUBLE MAKERS; it's the SDS!!!" etc.

I do not feel the SDS or communists had much, if anything, to do with Kent or any of the other universities. People cannot understand that the youth actually feel something is wrong in this country and are trying to make all others see the error so we may change it.

It seems as if the U.S., according to them, is perfect. The U.S is never the aggressor, never tries to force its ideas and philosophies on other nations, never does anything wrong. The U.S. doesn't go into towns and wipe villages out, not the U.S.! A Russian does, Communist Chinese do; all our enemies do. Don't we, too?

I am beginning to feel more and more trapped—our hometown newspaper ran a pledge asking for people's signatures against antiwar demonstrators, against long-haired hippies, against riots,

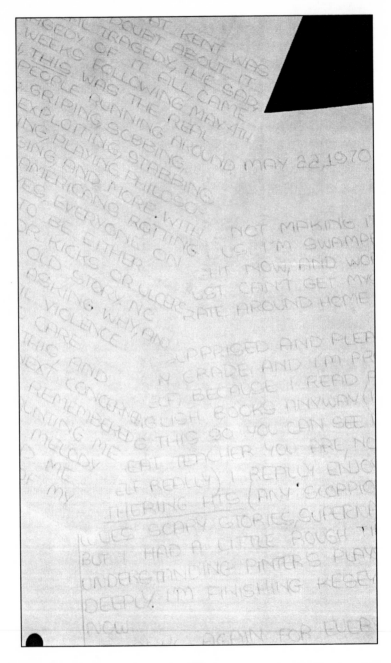

etc. Literally thousands of people signed it. I was shocked.

How can people believe that all people with long hair are bad? Many of them have never met or talked to a long-haired person in their lives, yet they hate them for their hair, not their personalities.

I am becoming more and more detached from my family. My parents lecture day and night. I cannot stand another lecture.

During the past few months I have grown up considerably. I am more confused than I was before, but at least I am thinking. I will return to Kent next September, sooner if possible.

Somehow the students and professors will pick up the broken pieces of a split university and try to glue it back together, hopefully better than it was before.

I will be sending a paper to you later on this week. Thank you so much for opening the doors for me into the humanities and great literature. Each quarter I come closer and closer to completely opening the doors to my curiosity, to try [to] understand people. . . .

Much love and many thanks,

J.C.

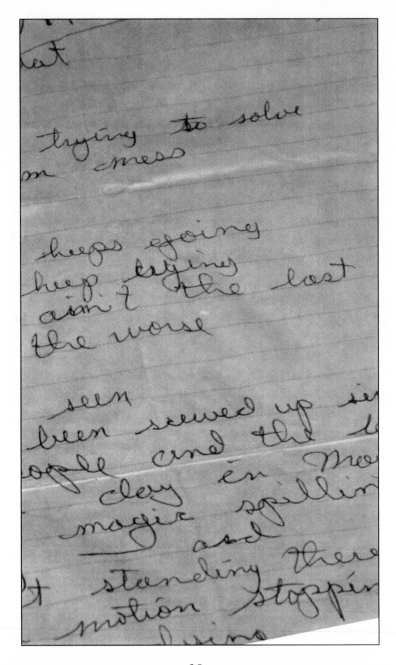

DISAPPOINTMENT

This weekend I manned a booth for the Multiple Sclerosis drive. It was a small booth at which we gave away balloons to kiddies in exchange for a contribution of any size.

Multiple Sclerosis is a crippler of many young adults. It goes through various stages and various degrees, impairing eyesight, speech, hand and leg movement, urinary control, etc. Any young adult is a liable victim of the crippler, and there is no cure or prevention as of yet.

I stood in front of the booth smiling as each person went by saying, "Would you like to contribute to M.S. research?" I began to get discouraged. People, literally hundreds of them, passed me by, yet only a few stopped to drop a few pennies in the collection tray.

I could see the guilty looks written on the children's faces, but they had no pennies. "Mommy" and "Daddy" were the only ones who did.

It would not have been so aggravating, but these same people who did not have a dime to help a crippled woman in the hospital, had a quarter to buy an ice-cream. Why can't people give a little to help others?

The same people who passed by were just the right age to get M.S., but of course, "nothing bad ever would happen to them." It still could strike them or their family, perhaps the nickel they would have given but did not, would have found the cure for this disease.

Are people so hardened today that they cannot help or think [of their] fellow man? Has the world come to such a state that the principle of a high school, the president of a bank cannot afford to spare a dime?

Why can't people take an extra second and with a smile say, "Yes, I'd love to contribute; thank you for asking."

J.C.

M.F.S. May 26, 1970 - CALIFORNIA

May 4, 1970

Monday, May 4, 1970, is a day for all students to remember. Some people were wrong, and some people were right, and the blame has been put on many fronts; but, regardless of the outcome, legally or morally many students and faculty members have been left with a picture of violence and death to remember for a long time.

I was not involved in the leadership of peace marches or protest rallies. I only participated in a rally on the commons Monday afternoon at noon. The rally started out peacefully, on both sides, but ended up a story to be told [to] your children. Both students and National Guard were aggravated and annoyed. The National Guard was annoyed by rocks and yelling students, while the students were aggravated by tear gas and marching uniformed men.

In my opinion, both sides were wrong, and the whole affair was very unreal. But when two sides are wrong, a person generally tends to find the side who is the most wrong. I feel that side was the National Guard officers and authorities. Maybe the National Guard was endangered by screaming kids throwing rocks from 25 yards away; but, a student's life is more in jeopardy by a bullet shot into a large crowd from 50 feet away.

Maybe I am being prejudiced and emotional, but when three acquaintances are killed and one very close friend is critically shot, I feel there is no other way to react. I have tried to reason out the answer,

and justify the shootings, but I can't seem to be able to do that.

Sometimes you have life all figured out and then one day it is all confusion again. I know I will never forget May 4th, but most of all I will never forget how the older generation let the students down in their ability to judge and react to a certain situation.

M.F.S.

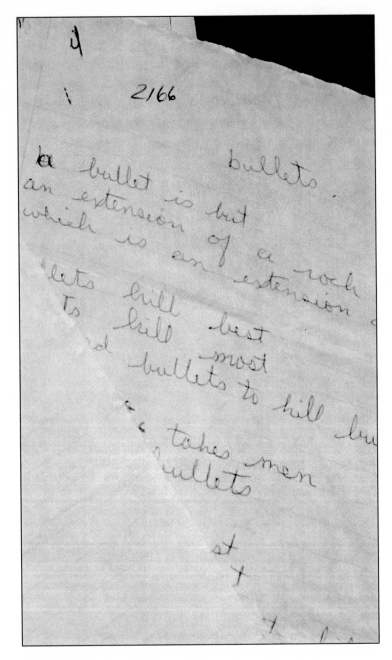

C.S. May 27, 1970 - Ohio

Rather than write a composition as such, I decided to write in the form of a letter to you.

I was not on the commons on that "black Monday." So I can't really comprehend the horror of what happened, but I keep asking myself why did those students have to gather when they were told there was to be no assemblage anywhere on campus?!

Mrs. Agte, Mr. Nixon is, in my opinion, a poor excuse for a President, and I'm totally against his policies, but I realize that law does exist, and it must be respected in order to prevent a more chaotic state than the one our country is in now!

At first I was in total defense of the National Guard. On the Saturday night that the ROTC building was burned down, I watched as students defied the Guard, yelling, laughing, and throwing rocks, as if it were all just a game.

The students who took an active part in the protests attempted to destroy the City of Kent on a Friday night and on the following Saturday, they rallied for peace and nonviolence. Aren't such actions rather hypocritical? ROTC is not mandatory at Kent State, and students are a part of it because they want to be! Why should this have been taken away from them?

My brother, a doctoral candidate, called the deaths at KSU "outright murder." He said there have been worse riots and they have been controlled without any lives lost. I am so very confused because I have my beliefs and yet, others' beliefs, such as my brother's make sense to me.

Unfortunately, there will always be two "stories" as to what happened at Kent, and we will probably never know the complete truth as to what really occurred, and why it did.

I just keep thinking, if the protestors and "curious onlookers," as the newspapers described them, had done as they were told—not to gather on the commons—four students would still be alive, and thousands of others would not be deprived of an education.

Do have a good summer. Take care and I hope to see you next fall.

Fondly,

C.S.

June 4, 1970 - Ohio
Second Letter from C.S.

Dear Mrs. Agte,

I wish to thank you for your moving letter and the copy of Yevtushenko's beautiful poem in memory of Allison Krause. Although Allison ate in my dorm, I never really got a chance to know her as a person. When I saw her and Barry together, Barry always smiled and said, "Hello," but Allison just stared at me.

38

Why? I don't know.

Many times I remained quiet in your class while Barry, Allison, and that boy that you seemed to know quite well, and who sat next to me—I have forgotten his name—discussed such topics as the war, Ralph Nadar, and statistics, etc.

Mrs. Agte, I never felt capable of taking a part in those discussions. I hate to say it, but perhaps I am a part of the silent majority. I just don't believe in violence, and so many protests, such as the one at Kent and those at Watts, end in tragedy.

That is why I have never taken an active part in a protest, and went to class as I normally would on Monday, May 4, 1970.

It is all so very tragic. The Guardsmen were wrong in firing. The students were wrong in throwing rocks, bottles, and sticks as well as in their attempt to destroy downtown Kent. I pity both sides. The Guardsmen assigned to Kent State have to live with a conscience. The students of Kent State now have only the memory of four fellow students, and perhaps, friends.

Yes, I plan on returning to KSU in the fall. Many of my friends aren't. Because of the tragic incidents, their parents have forbidden them to. Of course, I'm anxious to get back.

I'm sorry to say I won't be going back with the same anxiety I felt as a freshman in the fall of 1969, for the City of Kent and the University will never be the same. A certain, infinite sadness will always be present in the minds of students, professors, and I'm

al acti...
he ROTC building wa...
ren hack hoses in two and ...
calling in of police help was ...
n the destruction of Government
ment of National Guard troops was
the destruction of a fence around
e burning of a building used to
equipment and tennis scoreboards all
was a mob bent and on destruction
ment in Cambodia as an excuse.
destroyed troops would not have
monstrations been peaceful the events
he shooting and the shooting itself
occured. Curfews were legal and demo
not. The students brought a state of
martial law upon themselves.
events would not have occured if stud
ators and the curious had obeyed a la
sperse. The shooting was unexcuseable
iolence and the deaths of four student
volved in protest or not, was brought
neir fellow students.

Agte, these are the things I saw an
I will be in Kent in three weeks and
drop in and talk to you about our un
...vement in Indo-China.

Respectfully,

sure, many of those who merely live in the City of Kent and are in no way related to the school. Students and professors will also be bitter; businessmen will inevitably be hostile.

I now find myself in deep moods of depression quite often. I keep asking myself, why did it have to happen at Kent? My brother said, "AC., it had to happen somewhere. Perhaps now people will wake up and work for a better society and the abolishment of the great injustices in our government." I certainly hope he is right.

I realize that you are very busy, but I would love to hear from you. I'm so sorry I didn't get to know you better. You seem very warm, understanding, and kind. Your hospitality (the invitation to your home) is overwhelming.

I hope to come to your house once I return to school. Thank you. I miss you.

With fondness and deep respect,

C.S.

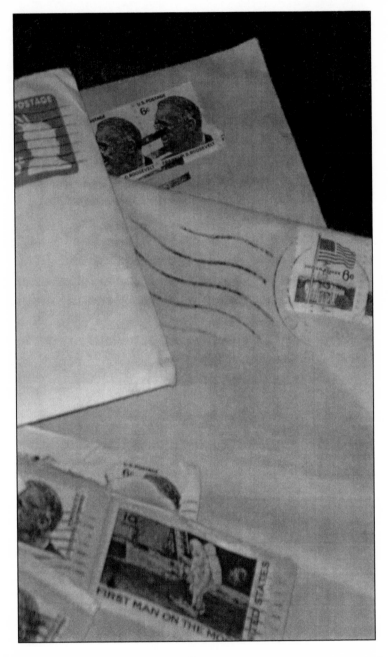

G.S. June 15, 1070 - OHIO

UNTITLED

The events which occurred on campus during the days of May 1-4, will be events which I shall never forget. I participated in the demonstrations during those four days and I was also there when the fatal shots were fired. On my way home, I was still quite dazed, but all I kept asking myself and my friends is why did all this have to happen at Kent? I was in favor of the demonstrations to try and get the students' point across. I was not at all in favor of any sort of violence. All I wanted to see was the demonstrations carried out in a peaceful manner. Nothing can be accomplished by violence.

After we were sent home on May 4, I decided to carry on my ideas of what the students were trying to accomplish at Kent to other college and high school students, plus the parents in my community. A few days after I was home, the faculty at my former high school asked me, and a friend of mine, who also goes to Kent . . . to come down and give our views on what had happened at Kent. After we related our feelings and ideas on what had happened, I thought only a few teachers really knew what we were trying to get across. As far as the students were concerned, they seemed interested, but I think they still think the occurrence at Kent had no direct influence on them, so why should they become involved.

I also went to Union College in Alliance, and

gave a talk there to only a handful of students.

As most people know, Mt. Union is one of the most conservative schools in Ohio. There, except for a few students, people would be more concerned with Mothers' Day on campus than what is going on around the rest of the nation on the college campuses. For example, 500 out of 1,200 students signed a petition to call for a campus strike, and only, at most, 50 students participated in the strike.

As far as the parents are concerned in my community, they believe what they want to believe. For the most part, they rely on a distorted mass-media's point of view of things. When a student tries to relate what is happening on college campuses around the nation, he is immediately stamped a radical if his ideas don't coincide with theirs. People in the community are really naive about things.

I don't know what to expect once we go back to school this fall. All I am hoping is that the students and the administration on the college campuses can unite their thoughts and make our nation and world a better place to live.

G.S.

P.F. July 21, 1970

MY COUNTRY TIS OF THEE,
SWEET LAND OF LIBERTY

American is not living up to its birthright. I mean where do racism, repression, hypocrisy, war, poverty, and murder come in? Since when does patriotism mean obedience whether right or wrong? Don't silent minorities belong in a dictatorship? I hold utmost contempt for the ignorance in this country.

The police state mentality of this nation is unbelievable. Nixon calling dissenting students bums, and in the same breath calling the boys in Vietnam a shining example: "They're just doing their duty." Their duty? Murdering and destroying—for what? The full-page ad in the Kent City newspaper thanking General Del Corso and the National Guard scares the shit out of me.

How can people be so ignorant? Since when is anybody thanked for murder?

I will never forget or forgive the first weekend in May. I remember coming back from town with some people Friday night. We were stopped in the street by seven pigs. One pig had a machine gun. I was overwhelmed.

I had never seen a machine gun except in the movies, and here I was standing in the middle of a street in Midwestern America looking at one. Wow! One of them said, "Halt." We were not aware anything happened that night. He said we could

...was the...
...right? That's sup...
rotten thing you have to...
guys are in the National Guard
love the military. They're there so...
of the draft and stay away f...
you are going to have to expect s...
but when trouble arises. But the...
should have had those powerful...
ridiculous, especially with so m...
standing there watching. I think...
should have had blanks and i...
kind of less powerful ammunit...
don't know what I would ha...
their position.

not go down the street.

I asked, "Why?"

He said there was a curfew law. Maybe I was naive, but I thought curfew was a time one had to be off the streets. I asked what time the curfew was. He answered, "Look smart ass, the curfew is you do what we tell you to do or we bust you." I told him I thought that sounded fair and that Hitler would be proud. We took a detour.

Cambodia really messed my head up. I did not understand how America could carry on an aggressive and colonial role in someone else's civil war, supporting a dictatorship, and invading a neutral country and putting up with a President who told us all we were there defending freedom.

The weekend of police repression aimed at stifling political dissent did not help my head either. Later that night, I saw tanks and half-tanks, and trucks and jeeps of troops rolling into Kent, invading our campus. And Sunday night the pigs lied to us. They told us that if we got out of the street and on campus, they'd remove the National Guard from front campus and bring the Mayor and President White to talk to us.

When the majority of students reached the campus, the rest in the street were busted, and the pigs surrounded us on front campus tossing tear gas canisters and waving clubs. I saw one chick bayoneted—many were clubbed.

While all this was going on, we were being called bolsheviks by Spiro Agnew, Martha Mitchell, and James Rhodes.

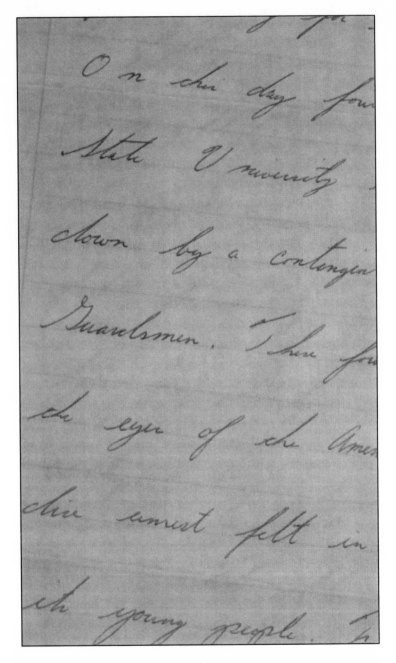

Monday. Christ . . . I was 70 feet from the guard contingent on the knoll right in the middle of the hill. I remember thinking that the shots sounded like toy guns; but I could see them pointing at us; but I kept thinking they had to be blanks, they had to be; but as I turned to run, the face of the boy in back of me exploded into flesh and blood. (Later I found out it was Jeff Miller.) As I watched him fall into the street, I just collapsed to the ground, sickened and shocked.

A kid right above me fell. I watched his shoe get shot off his foot. Somebody screamed to my left. I saw more blood. I watched the looks of terror and panic on the faces of the children crawling up the concrete side of Taylor Hall—crawling up to the trees. I heard screams of anguish and pain. Oh, Jesus—can I ever forget?

The shooting stopped. I slowly got up. We tried to help Jeff, but he was dead. A contingent of guard came over from the other side of Taylor. People were begging for help, but they kept walking. Someone told me Allison was hit. I ran up to see her taken away. We were with her at Tri-Towers the night before.

My head was not together. I just turned away—something snapped in my head. The guard contingent (wearing their gas masks) stopped at Jeff's body. I started screaming, "You murdered them," over and over, "You fucking fascist pigs. Why?"

Everybody was yelling. The guard then threw some type of gas on Jeff's body to disperse those around him—how grossly obscene.

I really don't blame the guard itself. They were scared. I remember how they were trembling on Saturday and Sunday night with loaded weapons. But will those murdering red-necked pigs Del Corso and Rhodes pay? I indict those two as well as I censure Agnew and Nixon for their aggressive policies, for their insensitive and arrogant administration.

My initial shock and despair [have dimmed], but I am left with frustration and anger. We thumbed to Washington on May 9 to demonstrate outside The White [House] with tens of thousands of other people who still believed there was something left of a democracy in this country. There was a ring of interlocking busses around the White House, and beyond the busses, rows and rows of troops. There were troops in windows of all the buildings, troops on the rooftops.

America. It was so ironic. How many more Kent States will there be? I can't believe the people just sat back and excused the murders of four adolescents. There is not much of a system left in this country to work through for results . . . so another way must and will be found to end the monstrosity that is American society. We must put an end to an immoral and an aggressive role and Southeast Asia and end the poverty, racism, repression, and hypocrisy that is America.

The current trend in this country is one of dehumanization and a swing to the far right.

Joe McCarthy would be thrilled. Both the public support of politically astute construction workers, who beat dissenters, and the public condemnation of students at Kent with a "they deserved it attitude" are horribly wrong and insane.

But I hope for peace, not only the obvious meaning of no more war but an inner peace in man so that he will not be uptight over whether a person is an American, a Russian, Chinese, a Swedish person or whether one is rich or poor or a Moslem, or a Jew, or Catholic, a Protestant, or whether one is a member of the silent majority or of the Woodstock Nation. We are all humans, and we must love one another.

I'm sorry this is so late, but I've had a lot of hassles lately. I've been in Canada for a while. Thanks for everything.

Peace,

P.F.

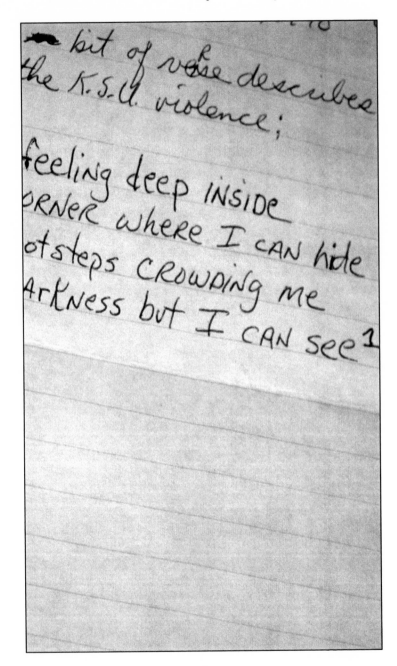

~ bit of verse describes
the K.S.U. violence;

feeling deep INSIDE
ORNER where I CAN hide
otsteps CROWDING me
ArKNess but I CAN see [1]

T.S.

Dear Mrs. Agte,

I am sorry things ended as they did for it was awful, and it was tragic to me especially since I knew the one young girl. I have tried to find explanations, but I can't. The town where I live is old fashioned and [people] resent the youth. Some will listen, but only for a while—a minute or so.

I did not want to write about the war or protest due to my emotions and inability to say properly what I really feel. I am frustrated.

Instead, I decided to write about the environment because I am working at a steel factory. The pollution is terrible. Another reason is through reading publications put out by the State of Pennsylvania. I have found that my home town of 25,000 people has the highest percentage of pollution by weight. Our pollution particles are heavier in suspension than both Pittsburgh and Philadelphia. That's bad. Something has to be done.

Thank you for listening to me. I hope you won't mind if I look you up next fall.

Yours in brotherhood and peace,

T.S.

POEM TO THE ENVIRONMENT

In the beginning God created the Earth
And the Earth had clean air,
Then came man
And Sin entered this beautiful paradise
All under the title of Progress

Soon man was destroying his forests,
Washing his land away,
And marring the landscape
With dead bodies
All under the title of Progress

Then came the populating of the whole world
And the destroying of more land,
the building of buildings,
And the birth of industry
All under the title of Progress

Now man's inventions and industries
Are poisoning our air,
Destroying clean water,
And corroding our landscape
And, of course, all under the title of Progress.

but soon man will die from this,
And all will be in vain
because the Progress will deteriorate
And the mortician will have to work—Overtime!

D.W. 7-17-70

THE COLLEGE CAMPUS

The college campus is not a place were violence should be utilized. The tragedies of Kent State and Jackson State College have proven this point.

Whenever there is a violent demonstration on a college campus, it warrants some form of government troops to the scene. The presence of these troops always seems to bring on even more violence, which involves the endangering of the students' lives.

When the ROTC building was burned down to the ground at Kent State University, Ohio State Police and Ohio National Guardsmen were immediately ordered to the area. The students did not appreciate the presence of fifteen hundred troops on the Kent State campus. Not only this, but the troops did not appreciate the demonstrations of students. The friction built up between both sides proved to be fatal for the students.

There are two classifications of people employed in government troops who do the killing. The first is the type of guy who is a scared soldier. He is scared for a few reasons: one reason being that he may get killed in the action, and the other being that he is holding a gun and he may have to kill someone.

The second classification is the soldier who is actually into "taking care of long-haired trouble makers." Regardless of his classification, these soldiers are extremely capable of killing and will continue to do so if put in a similar situation as those in Kent

and Jackson State. Because of this, situations of these types should be avoided.

The six lives lost in the week of May 4, 1970 at Kent State University and Jackson State College were unjustified deaths; they were a prime example of the powerful military the United States has at the head of her command.

Students should not go down to the low level used by government forces. Violence will only bring on more student deaths. Change has to take place by peaceful methods because the violent methods have already proven to be fatal.

Things such as campaigning for candidates to public office, petitions, student boycott of classes, economic boycotts, and other means, are peaceful ways which hopefully will bring about the change and improvement that we need in this country. If these peaceful methods fail and the frustration leads to violence, then the students of the United States and all other peaceful groups will be living in a sad situation.

D.W.

F.C. May 26, 1970 - OHIO

THE TRAGEDY AT KENT

My own views on the current unrest on the Kent State Campus are that the spirit of inquiry and understanding of issues central to the purpose of a university cannot be fostered by mindless violence and mob hysteria.

I think that the problems currently besetting the University can be resolved in a civilized manner by insuring that channels for dialogue are open at all levels on our campus, so that polarization of individual groups never reaches the extent that we become subject on the one hand to violent protest instant demand, and on the other, to the use of military force as a desperate measure to counteract possible threats to lives and property.

I, like everyone, abhor the use of violence such as the war in Vietnam, but I feel as a citizen of the United States we should stand behind our President in this war.

At least, give him some time to prove to us that what he is doing is right or maybe wrong before we judge him. I would certainly fear being under communist rule.

I enjoy the freedoms of speech and religion that we presently have in this country.

My parents work hard so that I can get an education, and now with the burning and destruction of our college buildings, it will certainly be another added burden to their taxes.

I feel that the minority groups started this trouble, and it is about time we heard from the majority.

Good luck and thanks,

F.C.

T.J. May 26, 1970 - Wisconsin

Dear Mrs. Agte,
 I really appreciate the A in English. It saved me a lot of work. I am still a little shocked at what happened May 4. I just hope that it never happens again. I wrote a little poem. It's not the best, but I think it has a lot of meaning.
  I'll see you next year.
   Thanks, T. J.

People want to be heard
but are as helpless as birds,
They tried marchin' and talkin'
but only heard Richard speakin!

Then they turned to violence and rage
As they all seemed to set the stage
For the NIGHTMARISH MAY 4 AT KENT STATE
Where 4 HELPLESS STUDENTS MET THEIR FATE.

These students were just lookin' on
And had no idea their lives would soon be gone.
They watched as others threw rocks
At the guard who were in a state of shock.

"Rocks can kill" they said
As they shot these four dead.
Their lives were at stake
Says who, for God's sake.

T.J.

L.G. June 10, 1970 - Ohio

Dear Mrs. Agte,

I was very glad that you took the time to write us students and explain your feelings about what happened on our campus. I have received many form letters from all of my professors, but your letter did much more than theirs. I truly believe your letter came through as an honest expression of your true feelings concerning the shootings that took place. For taking the time to express your feelings, and giving me more insight into what actually happened, I thank you!

Throughout last year I became concerned with student government at Kent. I realize that there are many who believe that any and all effective change can only be achieved through means outside of the system, or perhaps through means that are not peaceful. And, of course, I might add that our national government does have many faults and is plagued with a good deal of corruption.

Hypocrisy and hate are two very unpleasant words that describe the characteristics of too many of the people in our country. And may I point out that President Nixon and our Vice President have done more than their share to support violent means for achieving tangible results. By ignoring over one hundred thousand people who marched on Washington D.C. in November, the path for violence was made clear.

The President watched television (a football

game) and our Vice President called the demonstrators queers, etc.

Had our leaders done then, at least some of what they began to do following the KSU tragedy, perhaps then much of what has happened since November could have been avoided. The loud minority of students (ages 18-21) became a striking majority when placed in the armed forces and taken out of the perspective of the entire population. And it is within our armed forces that men will die, having never been given the opportunity (through the ballot or system) to help formulate those ideals for which they fought!! Is that justice? How can they help but feel disenfranchised?

Getting back to my original statement, I started to work somewhat with student government at K.S.U. I am presently running for the position of student senator. I realize that there is much against me, and of course, I had time to do only half of my campaigning prior to the closing of the university. If, however, I am elected to this position my concern rests with those of the students.

Many students feel that through our own student government nothing can be accomplished, and perhaps they are right. But I am attempting to do what I can regardless of the odds against my attaining success in the hopes that perhaps there remains a chance of our system working!

Mrs. Agte, you have quite a capacity for understanding and caring. I hope that, whether or not I make it to the position of senator, you will be willing perhaps to help us on some committees and in the formulating of our goals. Please tell me, do you feel that hope still exists through our university, or have you become disenchanted with the system to the point where you feel our only hope is through other means? What, if anything, do you feel our student government should become especially concerned with when it reconvenes in the fall quarter? And what can I do to help?

If you ever have some spare time (and of course, none of us ever really has any "spare" time), I would appreciate your suggestions and comments. I hope that in some way I can help us avoid future tragedies such as at K.S.U., but of course, I am only one person and then only a student. But I just can't say, "Well, that's it T., give up!" Thank you again for taking the time to read this letter. Best of luck with your next classes!

Yours truly,
June 10, Ohio

L.G.

C.G. 5/27/70 - Pennsylvania

Dear Barbara,

Wow, I really appreciated receiving your letter. You are the only one of my teachers who actually took time to write a letter. Since I feel so much for what happened at Kent, the only problem I will have writing a paper is time. But I will do it, and send it to you as soon as I can. Also an A as a final grade is fine with me. I would very much like to visit Allison's parents, and I plan to sometime before I leave Pittsburgh for the summer. Thanks again for your letter.
C.G.

C. G. 6/13/70 - Pennsylvania

Dear Barbara,

Sorry it took me so long to do this paper. I guess I was trying to put off thinking about what happened again for as long as I could. Anyway, the only thing I could write was how I feel. You're one of the few people that can understand me and other students, and therefore, you are one of the few who can understand what I've tried to say in my paper.

Peace,

CHANGE

It took me over a week to get my mind in some kind of organization after the Kent incident. After being home and talking to people, both for and against student demonstrations, I still have not been able to justify in my mind a reason for murdering four students.

My first reaction after the shooting was complete shock and mental disorganization. I just stood there, in the practice field and watched everyone running and heard the screaming. I had to leave.

I could not conceive of what had happened. It was like a war, but not a war of one army against another. It was a war between two contrasting views on government policies.

A war of one armed government organization against those strongly opposed to what that organization stood for. I don't care what anyone says, throwing stones is no provocation for murder.

At home, I wanted to talk and even scream a little to everyone I came in contact with. I was very restless. In my mind, I felt that what happened had a very definite purpose: to let everyone know what was going on and why is was happening.

My parents were my first objective. I had to let them know how I felt and why. They were very sympathetic toward me and other students. They, too, were against Nixon's Cambodian policy and finally understood that students demonstrations were letting Nixon and his administration know how people felt.

Violent arguing was also a part of my homecoming. I went to see an old friend. Although she was sad about the murders, she was violently against students' demonstrating.

I honestly felt sorry for her. She completely shut out everything that exists beyond the community we grew up in.

I can't help feeling if she had left home and gone away to school, her views on students' demonstrating would be completely changed. Neighbors, too, argued with me. I almost cried when a man I have known for ten years said, "If I had been there, I would have taken a machine gun and shot everyone of those demonstrators."

There were those who made me feel good and helped me regain hope for humanity. A woman I had never seen before looked at me very seriously and said, "Students know what they want; don't stop fighting." A local radio station held a poll on the question, "Should the National Guard fire on demonstrating students?"

Although thirty-eight were in favor and only eighteen opposed, the announcer was one who made me feel good. He was strongly against the Guard, and voiced his disgust with those who voted "yes". I was happy with him, but I cried for those who voted "yes" and [cried] with those who voted "no".

After all, this has been over for a month, my only hope is more people realize how bad our government is. How good can a government be if it starts killing students? I have gone through mental agony. If no one, or nothing else was changed by what happened at Kent, I've changed.

C.G. Pennsylvania

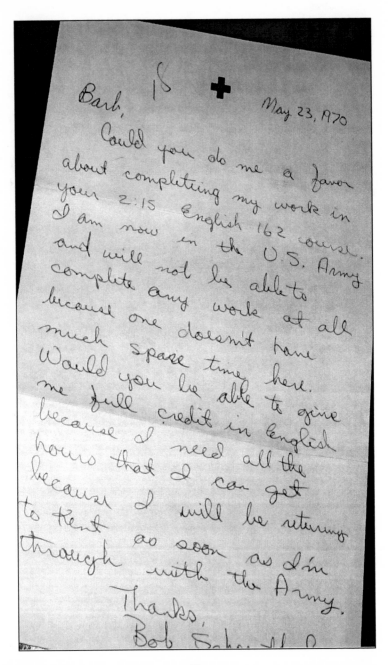

Barb,   May 23, 1970

Could you do me a favor
about completing my work in
your 2:15 English 162 course.
I am now in the U.S. Army
and will not be able to
complete any work at all
because one doesn't have
much space time here.
Would you be able to give
me full credit in English
because I need all the
hours that I can get
because I will be returning
to Kent as soon as I'm
through with the Army.
                    Thanks,
                    Bob _____

R.S. 4/23/70 - Kentucky

Dear Barb,

Could you do me a favor about completing my work in your 2:15 English 162 course. I am now in the U.S. Army and will not be able to complete any work at all because one doesn't have much spare time here.

Would you be able to give me full credit in English because I need all the hours I can get. I will be returning to Kent as soon as I'm through with the Army.

Thanks,

R.S.

P.S. I'll send you my permanent address so you can reply to me here.

I'll receive it in about a week.

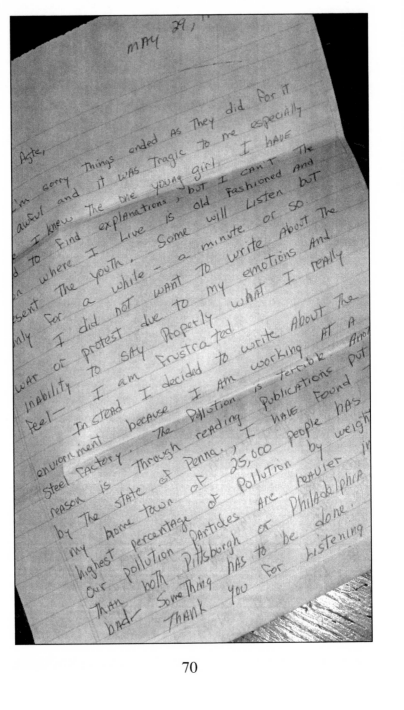

May 29, 19

After,

I'm sorry Things ended as They did. for it

was awful and it was Tragic to me especially

I to knew The one young girl. but I can't The

d to Find explanations, old Fashioned And

sent where I Live is Some will Listen but

nly for The youth. a while - a minute or so. The

WAr or I did not want To write About The

Inability to protest due to my emotions And

Feel - I am To say Properly what I really

Instead I am Frustrated

environment because I decided to write About The

Steel Factory. The Pollution is terrible At A

reason is Through reading Publications I have Found

by The state of Penna., 25,000 people has

my home town of Pollution by weigh

highest percentage Particles Are heavier

our pollution both Pittsburgh or Philadelphia

Than Some Thing has to be done.

bad Thank you for Listening

E.A. June 10, 1970 - Ohio

Mrs. Agte,

I'm really sorry I didn't get a chance to reply right away, but I was so busy trying to finish my other courses and work at the same time. In fact, as you probably can tell, I'm working right now. That's where I got the weird paper, and the dust finger-prints. [the student's letter is written on the back of a "performance report" form] I work in a sintering plant where they make dust, and heat; I guess.

I was going to come up to visit with you, but I had to work.

Tuesday, my cousin and I went to Columbus on our cycles, and Wednesday morning, 2:00 a.m. we decided to leave for Cleveland where my cousin lives. I stayed there [some crossed out words] till noon then took off for my home, and on the way went through Kent.

I tried to find where you lived, but all the money I had was 50 cents and I needed that for petro. I tried to get credit for a dime from the operator, but it didn't work.

The poem written by the Russian about Allison was quite impressive & makes one think before he or she sings the national anthem.

You wrote that you would like a poem or some other thing to finish the course. Well, I'm not much of a poet or writer, so I think I'll just write down my philosophy of life, which sums up all the past events & the ones to come.

IF THERE IS SUCH A PLACE AS HELL WE'RE IN IT.

(And he sent me an original painting. A finger print in red iron ore)

I must add before I leave that I think your class was very interesting, and I learned deeper things than where to put a period and spell.

Till we meet again

A student & friend

E.A.

D.B. June 3, 1970 - Ohio

UNTITLED ESSAY

Since I've been home from school, everybody has asked me what happened at Kent. I'm getting kind of tired of hearing about it, but it did happen. The first thing I can say, there was no reason in the world for the National Guard to be carrying bullets as powerful as the M61. But I do think that the students of Kent asked for the trouble.

They pushed the National Guard a little too far. They say they were protesting against the National Guard's being on campus. Well, they asked for that, too. What was the reason for tearing up downtown Kent Friday night? That's supposed to be demonstrating I guess.

Another thing you have to realize is that those guys are in the National Guard not because they love the military. They're there so they can get out of the draft and stay away from Vietnam, so you are going to have to expect some panic on their part when trouble arises, but there is no way they should have had those powerful bullets. That was ridiculous, especially with so many people just standing there watching.

I think the National Guard should have had blanks, and if that didn't work, some kind of less powerful ammunition or something. I don't know what I would have done if I was in their position.

D.B.

M.W. June 3, 1970 - Ohio

Dear Mrs. Agte,

Thank you very much for the grade that you gave me in English! I was really sweating that stupid quality standards test that I would [have] had to take this fall in composition. I have really enjoyed your last two courses in English; I only wish more of my profs had your vision of the matters at hand.

I am sorry that this paper is late in arriving, but I just had my brace taken off my arm that I got from a car accident one week before school closed. It seems to be o.k. now but a little stiff. I have yet to decide whether or not to file suit.

I will be working this summer at a YMCA camp in Michigan on the supervisory staff. (Camp S., largest of its kind in the nation). I will be returning to Kent this fall, trying to get closer to getting that BS Ed. However, before school, I am going out West to see how schools, country, and life in general compare with the State of Ohio. I hope you enjoy your summer, whatever you might do. Thanks again.

Sincerely,
M.W.

WHY KENT STATE?

Peaceful Kent State University nestled in the verdant capaciousness of sylvan Summit County was perhaps one of the lesser-known universities with an enrollment [of] over twenty-thousand students in the United States. At least it was up until May, 1970. Catalyzed by a move by President Nixon to push troops into Cambodia for a mass offensive, students at Kent State as well other universities began to show disapproval by some form of dissent or demonstration.

At Kent State the apparent mood was disapproval and on the Friday night following the President's speech a cataclysm of events started with the rioting in downtown Kent. The rioting snowballed into the burning of the ROTC building, more rioting and the arrival of the National Guard, and ending with the death of four students and the wounding of fifteen others. The questions are why Kent State, were the killings necessary and who was in the wrong, the students or National Guard?

Although not an actual witness to the shootings on Monday, [I learned from] my younger brother who was standing not more than ten feet from one of the students who was killed. "It made me sick," he said. "Those damn pigs didn't have to fire on the students!"

My brother was really upset and upon returning home, and while the incident was still fresh in his mind, wrote a twenty-four-page report on what he saw and how he reacted for future reference. The general of the National Guard stated that his men are given so many hours of riot training every year.

Being a veteran and cognizant of how things are actually handled, I know General Del Corso is full of bullshit. Sure National Guardsmen are given

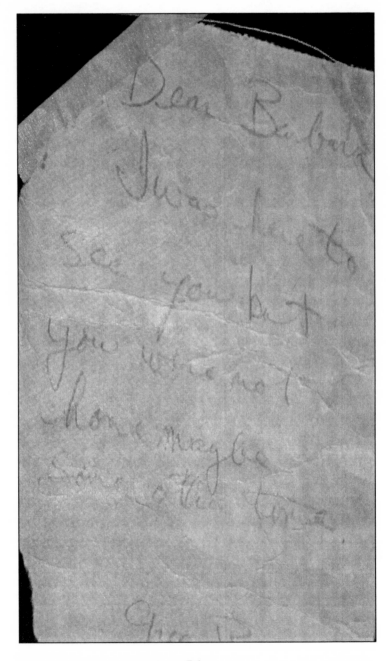

a block of instruction in riot control, but the training done is by an officer or a sergeant (with little knowledge about rioting) and is composed of mostly talking in a classroom to his men, who probably have a 50-70 percent attention span.

A practice session usually follows that, more often than not, turns into a horseplay session. Riot troops should be professionally trained men who know how to handle large masses of rioting people (students or otherwise) and be fully prepared to respond to any situation, resorting to firing only under extreme conditions.

The members of the National Guard were entirely out of order when they fired. However, what would have happened if they did not fire? Surely the guard would not have been over-run by the students . . . but who can say?

Evidently, whether at Kent State or another university, a similar incident probably would have happened, perhaps larger in magnitude. It is unfortunate though that it takes such a matter as killing to jar the [administration] of President Nixon and others and make them realize many students and citizens hate the damn war in Indo-China! Those who hate the war are tired of publically elected officials in local and national government who, when once elected, sit back in their chairs and get fat from the tax payer's money.

The time has come to drive a spike in the heart of congressional malingering and check this right now. By using activities whether in schools,

campaigning or just writing letters to your con-
gressman, these senseless nauseating events can be
stopped and the vomit that the government is spilling over its people can be irreversibly stopped, before some other mindless pig pulls a trigger.

M.W.

S.Z. May 24, June 4, 1970 - Ohio

THIS IS AMERICA

I am told that my desire to live should
be greater than my desire to die.
I am told that life is beautiful.
I am told that life is love.
I am told that what I really see, hear,
or feel is not truth but mere fallacy.
What, then, do I see?
What, then, do I hear?
What, then, do I feel?

I see Christians hate their fellow man.
I hear blacks preach equality yet discriminate
     amongst themselves.
I feel the heartache of love rejected.
I hear people slandered by their friends.
I see age take hold of people and rob them of their
     happiness.
I hear journalists take the oath of sensationalism.
I see young people murdered because they seek a
     change, because they seek peace.
I feel deep remorse for a democracy
     that will not listen to the voice of the people.
I see a person's worth measured, not by what he is
     but what he has.
I feel dismay in a religion practiced by hypocrites.
I see the prejudice of social workers.
I see patriotic Americans destroy their homeland

with pollution.
I hear the voice of young Americans
    smothered by the hands of tyranny.
I see President Nixon desecrate the constitution
    while a nation of imbeciles applaud him.
I feel compelled by society to adhere
    to its horrendous work ethic.

I see honest men step over others to reach the top.
I feel despair because I was born in a nation where
    people don't give a damn.
I see;
I hear;
I feel;
I die;
This is America!

S.Z.

D.G. May 26, 1970 - Ohio

GOVERNOR RHODES' FAULT

When the guard came to Kent, I didn't know who was responsible for their being there. I went to Miami University that weekend and when I returned to school, all I saw was guardsmen. I figured President White requested the National Guard. In listening to news reports and reading the paper, I found out that President White wasn't even at Kent that weekend. When he arrived at the airport, Governor Rhodes met him there and stated,"You've got trouble here."

Rhodes didn't tell President White that a state of emergency had been declared. Mr. Rhodes had to leave immediately for Columbus. Rhodes left Kent in charge of the National Guard. I blame Governor James Rhodes for the deaths of the four heroes at Kent.

President White is not to blame, for he couldn't even leave his house. The President should be criticized, however, for not communicating with his faculty from the time he arrived until Monday. The faculty didn't know what to do basically because President White didn't know what to do.

Some say the students antagonized the guard and forced them to shoot, for their own protection. This is complete garbage. The students were also accused of throwing rocks, and in some cases bricks. Later it was found out that all the students were throwing was clumps of dried mud, which certainly are not going to kill someone.

Finally, many students center the blame on the guard. Blaming the guard is like blaming the troops in Nam. Nixon is the one to blame for Vietnam, not the individual men. The guard didn't want to be in Kent; it was Rhodes' decision. Those guardsmen are only kids like us. Most of the guardsmen I spoke to were really great guys. Some pig gave the order to fire. I just know it!

From everything said so far, I really can't blame anyone but Rhodes. Last week I read in the paper that a student in California lit himself on fire to protest Nixon's policy in Vietnam. I can understand why that kid killed himself. He was just disgusted with the people in government, the big men, the pigs, the way I am.

D.G.

C.K. May 25 - Ohio

Dear Barb,

Thanks for not making it too rough on us. I'm swamped with art right now, and working, too. I just can't get myself to concentrate around home either. I was surprised and pleased about my grade. And I'm proud of myself because I read all my English books anyway. (I'm saying this so you can see what a great teacher you are, not for myself really.)

I really enjoyed *Wuthering Heights*. (Any Scorpio loves scary stories, [and tales of] supernatural.), but I had a little rough time understanding Pinter's plays very deeply. I am finishing Ken Kesey's book now. Thanks for everything, good luck, peace.

P.S. If possible, could I get this paper back? It isn't really important, but I'd like to have it.

UNTITLED ESSAY

What happened at Kent was a tragedy, no doubt about it. But the real tragedy, the sad, sick tragedy of it all, came in the weeks following May 4th. Oh, yeah, this was the real tragedy: people running around screaming, griping, sobbing, swearing, exploiting, stabbing, hating, acting, playing, philosophizing, nagging, and more. With four young Americans rotting in their graves, everyone on earth seemed to be either getting money or kicks or ulcers out of the same old story.

No voice was heard asking why, and no one

cared until violence made it popular to care. I was a part of this, and no better than the next "concerned citizen." I was, until I remembered the song that kept haunting me before the tragedy. The melody came to me and knocked me senseless during one of my own orations about Kent; just a day or two after the incident I shut my mouth and listened to all the racket.

The following [is a] play for voices concerning all that I have felt and heard. The characters should appear (through their speech) as ludicrous and absurd as they were and are in real life. The guitar music from Simon and Garfunkle's "Bookends Theme"should be heard throughout the play, and the lyrics written by Paul Simon, and recited by AC, are a part of me, of my mind. They fit in rather ironically to the b.s. When I heard, and realized I wanted to scream over the crowd and din saying, "How young were those four who died!? Why didn't we do something? Why don't we know?"

A SHORT PLAY FOR VOICES
(Music - "Bookends Theme")

A: Oh, yeah, I was there I know what happened.

B: (blanks) It sounds silly, but that was my first thought . . .

D: Damn troublemakers . . .

E: I knew her. She was one of my best friends. . .

C: (Sincerely, solemnly, and sadly) Time it was .

F: My best friend, I'm crushed . . .

C: And what a time it was . . .

G: Why were they up there? Throwing rocks. . .

H: Well, if that was your husband up there. . .

C: It was. . .
A: Such an innocent girl . . . My best friend . . .
E: Her kitten . . .
D: They should have shot 'em all . . .
C: A time of innocence . . .
G: They had no right being there . . .
H: Under such strain . . .
I: Sniper fire . . .
C: A time of confidences . . .
J: They're killing us! ! !
b: I saw the bodies . . .
F: An honor student, and a very religious per-
       son, I might add . . .
C: Long ago it must be . . .
D: Said he looked like a girl . . .
I: The Governor will . . .
J: My God, my God . . . So then I . . .
C: I have a photograph . . .
E: A trail of blood . . . I saw his head explode . . .
D: Commies . . . Movin' in . . .
C: Preserve your memories . . .
F: A flower . . .
G: They were scared stiff. I would have done the
       same thing . . .
B: Cambodia . . . Everyone's scared of war . . .
       Don't wanna die.
C: They're all that's left you.
K: And in the news today, the coroner has an-
       nounced new findings . . .
            (Music fades and finishes.)

The End.

85

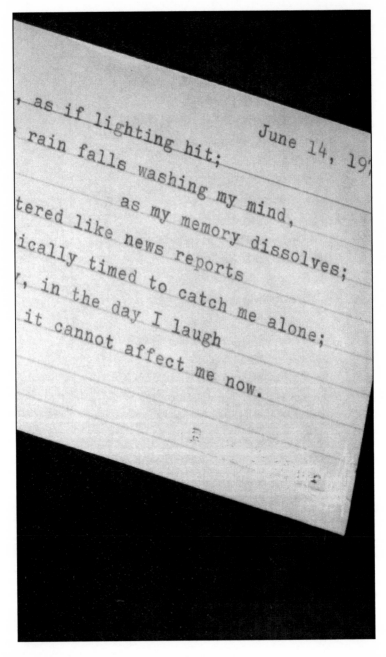

, as if lighting hit;
rain falls washing my mind,
June 14, 19

as my memory dissolves;
tered like news reports
ically timed to catch me alone;
, in the day I laugh
it cannot affect me now.

Barbara Becker Agte

R.G. June 5, 1970 - Ohio

POEM

Death is quick, as if lighting hit;
Days go by, the rain falls washing my mind
As my memory dissolves;
Flashbbacks scattered like news reports
Periodically times to catch me alone;
In the night I cry, in the day I laugh
I live so far away it cannot affect me now.

R.G.

GOD SAVE THE PEOPLE,
GOD SAVE THE COUNTRY,
GOD SAVE THE CHILDREN,
GOD SAVE US ALL.

POLLUTION, DISSENTION,
TAXATION, INFLATION
AND EVEN A WAR.

HELP THE PEOPLE REALIZE
THE YOUTH IS ON THE RISE.
GOD SAVE US ALL

THE YOUTH IS STEPPING FORWARD
OUR NATION IS HEADING BACKWARD
GOD SAVE THE MAN WHO ...
POOR

W.M. June 13, 1970 - New York

Dear Mrs. Agte,
      Please try and excuse the lateness of this paper. I did not receive your letter until Thursday, June 11. The mailman goofed and delivered it to the wrong house.
      I would like to say that I enjoyed our class discussions more than any course I had. I will not be returning to Kent due to insufficient funds. However, I will retain your address and if I am in the neighborhood, I will try and stop by. Good luck in the future.
      Sincerely,
      W.M.

UNTITLED POEM
God save the people,
God save the country,

God save the children,
God save us all.

Pollution, dissension
 Taxation, inflation
And even a war.

Help the people realize
The youth is on the rise.
God save us all

The youth is stepping forward
Our nation is heading backward
God save the man
   who will push the sacred button,
POOF, ...

W.M.

M.M. June 6, 1970 - Ohio

UNTITLED ESSAY

Were the events that led up to the shooting of four students at Kent State really necessary? The ultimate blame for the tragedy must be put on the students and non-students involved in the three days of childish and criminal actions of these misguided children.

The burning of the ROTC building was unforgivable and when these children hack hoses in two and throw rocks at firemen, the calling in of the police help was to be expected, and with the destruction of Government property the deployment of National Guard troops was inevitable. With the destruction of a fence around the commons and the burning of a building used to store intramural equipment and tennis scorecards, all I could envision was a mob bent on destruction using our involvement in Cambodia as an excuse.

Had students not destroyed [property], troops would not have [been] deployed. Had all demonstrations been peaceful the events leading up to the shooting itself would not have occurred. Curfews were legal and demonstrations were not.

The students brought a state of emergency and martial law upon themselves.

Monday's events would not have occurred if students, both demonstrators and the curious, had obeyed a lawful order to disperse. The shooting was

inexcusable but so were the actions of the students.

Violence leads to violence and the deaths of four students, whether involved in protest or not, was brought upon them by their fellow students.

Mrs. Agte, these are the things I saw and the way I feel. I will be in Kent in three weeks and I would like to drop in and talk to you about our university and our involvement in Indo-China.

Respectfully,

M.M.

T.P. June 12, 1970 - Ohio

Dear Mrs. Agte,

I'm sorry I got my paper in so late but I got a job and haven't had that much time.

After school was let out, a lot of people asked me what happened at Kent. Hearing people's reactions was pretty interesting; most were for the deaths, but these people are in the same rut they've been in for the past 40 years. People are really ignorant, and they displayed it when they said the guard should have shot. If only they were there and saw what happened.

One good thing was that G. and I were able to go speak to different classes at our high schools. Here reaction was mixed; some listened, others goofed around and will probably fall into that rut that most people fall into.

Well I've enjoyed being in English and I wish you peace and happiness in the years to come.

Love,

T.P.

UNTITLED ESSAY

May 4th, 1970 was a day of awakening for the United States. On this day four students at Kent State University were brutally gunned down by a contingent of National Guardsmen. The four deaths opened the eyes of the American people to the unrest felt in this country by its young people. Four deaths to show how concerned the future generation is for its country.

Most young people do not have anything to look forward to in life but to serve this country by fighting a war in a distant [land] to preserve liberty in the world. Why then must young Americans die in a fight for liberty when actually they have no liberty in their own country?

The older generation is really an obstacle to students. Without a voice in government, our [officials] make governmental decisions for the younger generation. The older generation isn't realistic [enough] to realize what has happened to the United States. The older generation with its unrealistic President sees fit to mold young people's lives for them.

Is it possible to open the ear of government with four deaths? What better example is needed to show our government a change is needed? There . . . changes young people wait for an attempt to change.

T.P.

M.G. May 27, 1970 - Ohio

Dear Mrs. Agte,

I am deeply upset by what has happened at
Kent State University. I hope peace can prevail in
the near future and that the university will function
again in its best possible ways.

I miss being in English class and seeing all the
fellow students and faculty.

Peace be with you. I hope all of us can return
again.

Sincerely yours,
M.G.

MY EVALUATION OF THE INCIDENT AT KENT

I do not believe it is right or possible to form a
hasty evaluation of what happened recently at Kent
State even though thousands of inches of newsprint
have been written, and even more words spoken
about the happenings and shootings at this university
which I attended the past year.

I made the above observation, first of all,
because the incidents are a part of a broader drama
of history which is being made in our time.

During the 1950s, it was said that college
students were rather silent, while in the 1960s and in
the beginning of the present decade, they are quite
active.

This activity has been and is being observed on
college campuses in various countries of the world,
and in our nation as well.

It has been said that students are restless because of war, and the failure of the so-called 'establishment' to do anything about it, as well as the other social, political, and economic ills of our time.

They see things happening to our country that are weakening and destroying it.

Even in our colleges and universities the students feel that faculty and administration members do not care enough.

From what I have observed on our campus and read, I feel that most of our students were there to study and to get an education.

Most of our faculty and administration members are sincere and dedicated.

I personally, however, would welcome stricter supervision of students in dormitories, etc. . . . I also have drawn [the] conclusion to the effect that some of our faculty members are somewhat "left of center"in some ways.

I deeply feel that in spite of some of my concern about our school, it is most unfortunate that a 'black mark' has been given to our college. It will take years for it to recover from this blow.

It would appear from newspapers and other sources that the students alone were not responsible for the disturbances. Outside influence apparently was there.

I hope the public, therefore, is fair in [its] evaluation of what happened at Kent State.

While I don't know all the facts, I do feel that the National Guard was also at fault. It lacked discipline, training, and equipment.

Kent State is still a school dedicated to the teaching and training of youth to serve our country in many ways.

I hope that this sad chapter in the glorious history of our school will move and motivate all of us to try and correct the evils which plague our country and society.

In the forefront of this movement must be our colleges and universities. We students must work along with them. Both groups need each other more than ever.

To this goal I pledge myself anew.
How about you?

M.G.

P.D. Left in door, June 1970 - OHIO

EPITHET

O.K. now
like I've been trying to solve
and I can't

but the mess keeps going
and people keep lying
and Kent ain't the best
and I guess the worse

worst I've seen
man I've been screwed up since
bleeding people on the lawn
a beautiful day in May
blood so magic spilling and
splashing C. and
me, just standing there
things in motion stopping
things inside dying

so I guess now I
just want out of the
country

or fly on a razor blade's kiss
with an epithet
written on the toilet bowl,
"Fuck it".

BULLETS

a bullet is but
an extension of a rock
which is an extension of the fist

bullets kill best
bullets kill most
we need bullets to kill bullets

but it takes men
to fire bullets
and truly
men kill best
men kill most
we need bullets to kill men

but we do
and children too

and not everyone uses bullets
but everyone is a murderer

P.D.

C.H. June 13, 1970 - Ohio

Dear Barbara,

I regret having to send my paper in this late, but I have been working and trying to finish my studies at the same time. I hope that my paper will be sufficient to fulfill the requirements for English 162.

I am hoping that I shall have the opportunity of having you as my instructor again. I found our class discussions most interesting and thought provoking.

I hope we can still keep in touch, and also if you are ever near my home, please feel free to stop in.

Sincerely,

C.H.

STUDENT UNREST AT K.S.U.

Since the tragic weekend of May 1st at Kent, I have been totally confused as to my future as a student at Kent and as a U.S. citizen. In trying to fulfill both these positions, am I obligated to condone the murders among my fellow students at Kent and also among fellow men in Cambodia and Vietnam? Is this what is expected of me by government officials, parents, and other adults?

For weeks after incidents at Kent and other college campuses, my brother (a sophomore at the University of Dayton) and I held heated discussions with our parents and relatives. Of course, my brother and I supported the students; our parents and relatives sided with the National Guard and other law officials. After awhile, I felt as if our opinions were nothing, because the adults are always right and never wrong.

I felt as if some of the student rallies that weekend were justified. Although I am not in agreement with student destruction of city and university property,

I do feel the incidents of Friday and Saturday night aided in building up tension against law officials. I believe the actions of students on these two days served the purpose of protesting U.S. involvement in Cambodia.

But I, as many other students, felt that some student arrests were ridiculous. These arrests seemed to be unjustified since the students themselves did not know what they had done wrong. Some of my friends were arrested for so-called curfew violations, and they weren't even aware of a curfew on the campus or city. Is this justice?

It seemed to me the rallies of Sunday night and Monday were held mainly to protest the presence of the National Guard on the Kent campus.

I, myself, was upset over their presence. I felt as if I was in the midst of a war—the major object of the student protest. How could peace possibly have been brought to our campus under such conditions?

Monday, May 4th, became a tragic day with the loss of four lives from one big family at Kent.

Little did I know that such an incident would occur at K.S.U. but in my eyes, those four students

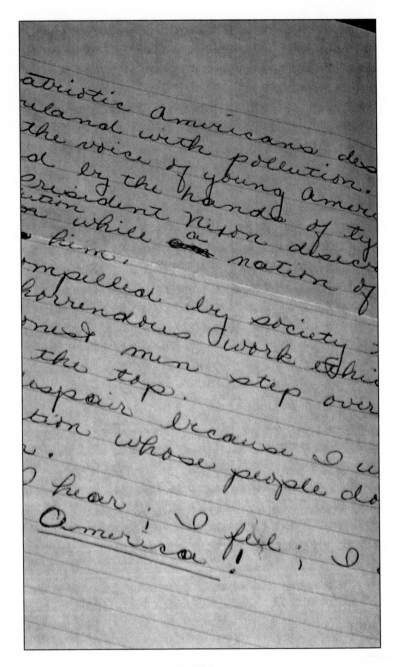

atviotic Americans de
land with pollution.
the voice of young Ameri
d by the hands of ty
President Nixon disc
n while a nation of
him.
mpelled by society
horrendous work eth
must men step over
the top.
espair because I w
tion whose people do
I hear; I feel; I
America!!

have become heroes and heroines of our country.

Through them, student voices were heard and finally our opinions were recognized. For this moment, a generation gap did not exist.

C.H.

END OF STUDENTS' LETTERS

Flowers & Bullets
by Russian Poet
Yevgeny Tevtushenko

[©New York Times Service Translation]

Anyone who loves flowers
    Is naturally not liked by bullets
Bullets are jealous ladies. Can one expect
kindness?
Nineteen year old Allison Krause,
You were killed because
You loved flowers.
It was
An expression of purest hopes
In the split second
    When defenseless as
        The thin pulse of conscience
You placed a flower
    In the barrel of
        The Guardsman's rifle.
And said:
    "Flowers are better than bullets."
Don't give a gift of flowers to a state
    Where truth is punished.
The response of such a state is cynical and cruel
And that's what the response was
    to you,
Allison Krause,
Bullets,

Pushing out the flower.
Let all the apple trees of the world,
    Not in white—
        But in mourning be clothed.
Ah, how sweet the lilacs smell
    But you don't feel anything.
As the President said about you,
    You are a "bum."
Every dead person is a bum,
    But this is not his fault.
You lie in the grass
    With a candy stick in your cheek.
You won't put on any new clothes,
    You won't read any new books.
You were a student
    You studied the fine arts
But there is another art—
    It is bloody and terrible
In this hangman's art
    There also obviously
        Are geniuses.
Who was Hitler?
    A Cubist of new gas chambers.
In the name of all flowers
    I curse your creations
You architects of lies,
    Conductors and murders,
Mothers of the world moan:
    "O, God. O, God."
And fortune tellers are afraid
    To predict the future.

At this moment, a rock and roll
    Of bones
    I'd danced by death in Vietnam
        And Cambodia.
And what theatre
    Will it find tomorrow
        To perform in?
Rise, girls of Tokyo
    Boys of Rome,
Gather flowers
    Against the evil enemy of all.
Blow together on all the dandelions
    Of the world—
O, what a great storm there well be!
Flowers, gather for war!
    Punish the oppressors!
One tulip after another
    One daisy after another
Burst forth in anger
    From tidy gardens,
Stuff with earthy roots
    The throat of all hypocrites
You, the Jasmine, clog
    The propellers of mine-layers.
You the nettles, stick firmly
    To the lenses
    Covering up the gun sights.
Get up lilies of the Ganges
    And the Lotus of the Nile—
And block the props of airplanes.
Pregnant with death of children

Roses, don't be proud
        Because they sell you
    For a little more.
Although it is nice to touch
    The tender cheeks of a
Young girl
Pierce
    The gas tanks
        Of bombers
With your thorns grown longer
    And sharper.
Against them you cannot rise up
        With flowers only
Their stems are too fragile—
    Their petals are a poor defense,
But a Vietnam girl—
        The same age as Allison—
    Taking in her hand a gun
Is an armed flower,
    The wrath of the people.
If also the flowers rise,
    Then it is no use
        To play children's games with
    History.
Young America,
    Tie up the hands of the killers.
Grow
    Grow
        The escalation of truth
Against the trampling
        of the life of people,

The escalation of liars.
Flowers, gather for war.
Defend beauty.
Flood the highways and byways
Like the menacing flow of an army,
And in the ranks of people and flowers
Rise up murdered Allison Krause,
Like the immortelle of the epoch—
The thorny flower of protest.

25 Years After

Kent State   *
May 4, 1995

25th Commemoration
Program

*
Photo by John Filo

May 3rd, 1995

- 11 am - 3 pm

  Informational Tables, Student Center Plaza
  *Current student activist groups display what they're
  doing to change the world today*

- 3 - 5 pm

  M4TF Picnic, Fred Fuller Park (Rt 59)
  Donations accepted

- 5 pm

  "We March With Them", Student Center Plaza
  *Student Activist March, bring your banners, slogans and
  favorite chants!*

- 6 pm

  "Kent State: A Requiem", KIVA
  *Performed by students from Emerson College,
  Boston, Mass*

- 7 pm

  **"Student Power: When students take a
  stand, students change the world"**, KIVA
  *Perceptions of student activism from past
  and present activists. Speakers include*

  - Mark Rudd - National SDS
  - Bill Whitaker - Kent SDS
  - Joyce Cecora -Kessler - Kent SDS
  - Ken Heineman - Author of *Campus Wars*
  - Paul Rogat Loeb - Author of *Generation at the Crossroads*
  - Alan Canfora - Wounded May 4, 1970
  - Sarah Lund - Student Action Coalition/M4TF
  - Stephanie Arellano - United States Student Assoc
  - Jeremy Smith - University Conversion Project

- 10:30

  "I Hear The Drumming", May 4th Memorial
  Informal gathering of local drummers

- 11 pm

  Silent Candlelight March, Commons

- Midnight

  Candlelight Vigil, Prentice Parking Lot
  *Start of 12 hour vigil in the places were the four
  students fell. To stand 1/2 hour vigil, please contact M4TF*

25th

Comm

Kent Sta

Ken

May 4th, 1995

• 8 am - 12 noon
Tours of May 4th Site
See M4TF Members at Williamson Alumni Center or Prentice Hall
Parking Lot

• 11:50 am
Gathering in the commons
• Magpie

• 12:24 pm
Ringing of the Victory Bell. Commons
*The bell is rung annually at the commemoration 15 times, 13 to
honor the KSU victims and 2 to honor the Jackson State victims*

• 12:30 pm
"In the footsteps of history, we march with them" Commons
25 annual commemoration event. Speakers include:

• Howard Metzenbaum, Former US Senator
• Paul Rogat Loeb, Author of *"Generation at the Crossroads"*
• Mark Rudd, National SDS
• Stephanie Campbell, Co-President M4TF
• Barbara Agte, Friend of Allison
• Steve Drucker, Friend of Sandy and Jeff
• Lou Cusella, Friend of Bill
• Chic Canfora-Knepp - Eye witness May 4th, 1970
• Peter Yarrow, Singer
• Sanford Rosen, Attorney
• Roland Colom, Jackson State
• Kermit Dilworth, Jackson State

• 3 pm
"Finding a Common Ground", Commons
A participatory public work of art dealing with negative space

• 3:45 pm
Student Activism Teach-in, KIVA
• Peter, Paul and Mary

• 7:30 pm
Benefit Concert
• Peter, Paul and Mary
• Special guests - The Murmurs
*Proceeds go to the May 4 Commemorative Student Activism
Scholarship Fund
(Tickets available though Ticketmaster)*

nual

ration

iversity

hio

Speech given
by
Barbara Agte

At

25th Commemoration
Kent State University
Kent, Ohio

May 4, 1995

12:24 p.m. Kent State University Commons

If I were a magician, suddenly, in the right hand of each of you, there would appear a flower—a wild flower—in the color which pleases you the most.

If I were a Buddhist teacher, I would suggest you look carefully at your flower and would say nothing further to you.

If I were John Donne, I would ask you to recall and hold in your heart, for these moments, the sound of the bells you have recently heard. And I would say, "Ask not for whom the bell tolls," saying next, "it has tolled for thee."

But I am a woman who, in the spring of 1970 was a teaching fellow in the Kent State English Department, blessed, as I had been each quarter, with wonderful students. Among those students, that spring, was Allison Krause, one of the 13 killed and/ or wounded here 25 years ago.

When Allan Canfora called to ask me to speak as a friend of Allison, and we continued to visit, I could not refrain from telling him how the foothills of the mountains near my home in the high desert of New Mexico were miraculously blanketed with millions of orange and yellow poppies. I told him that the desert was transformed and that the event had begun to transform the population. People from the cities were forgetting their business-as-usual and were coming in great numbers to see the wildflowers.

One old rancher who has been living in the desert for over 50 years said he had never seen flowers like those that appeared this spring.

And amazingly, the flowers had staying power. They lasted for well over a month and people who picked a few and took them home and put them in water learned the flowers lasted for up to seven days—something wildflowers generally do not do.

Flowers are always a special treat, but when they are found in places like the desert, they are a way, I believe, of the earth's reminding us that sometimes beauty and truth can be found in unlikely places.

When I think of Allison, I associate her with life, with sunshine, with truth, with flowers and especially with two books.

Some days I would get to our class a tad early and watch my students as they entered and settled themselves. It was a good time for me to greet them and speak with them individually. I remember one day watching Allison as she came in. She had her index finger in *One Flew Over The Cuckoo's Nest*, and she stopped to show me her book, and to tell me she was loving reading it. The book was on the syllabus, but the class had not yet begun reading and discussing it. She was reading ahead—something that always made my heart happy. I remember other days looking at her and thinking she had just washed her wondrous dark and wild hair. She was lovely— full of a strong life spirit. She spoke easily and kindly with others. And she joked in a loving way.

The last time I saw and spoke with Allison was Sunday, May 3rd. I had been at a meeting of faculty and teaching fellows, where 23 of us had signed a resolution proposed by Sidney Jackson, asking that the militia be removed from campus before its members brought harm to themselves or others.

The campus that Sunday seemed full of people. It was a beautiful sunshine-filled day, and there was a feeling among the people I met that "we would overcome."

I met Allison and her beloved companion, Barry, also a member of my class. They, primarily Barry I believe, told me how Allison had put flowers in the barrel of a gun a guardsman was holding, saying to him, "Flowers are better than bullets." I remember thinking, how brave! How brilliant! How wise!

Allison and Barry led me over to the guardsman who had been told by a superior to remove the flowers. He smiled at us all; we at him.

116

He blushed and I thought how young; how like a new toy he looked.

In preparation for meeting you today to speak of Allison, I reread *One Flew Over The Cuckoo's Nest*. Also, I read *The World of Oz* because Barry and Bonnie, another special friend to Allison, had told me Oz was her favorite book and film.

Reading first Cuckoo and then Oz, I've been realizing how alike the two books are—how they both speak of life, of kindness, of innocence, of true friends, and how necessary those elements are to us all to face terror we do encounter.

Joseph Campbell, in *The Power of Myth*, speaks of a Picasso engraving in which a raging minotaur has entered a circus. A frightened philosopher has climbed a ladder for safety. In the circus ring, there is a dead horse and a dead rider. There only person facing the minotaur/bull monster is a young girl with a flower. Campbell believes the engraving illustrates the "problems of modern day."

Allison's putting the flowers into the barrel of a guardsman's gun and telling him, "Flowers are better than bullets," is the 1970 living version of Picasso's engraving. Her action was a startling confrontation between innocence and organized state-sanctioned force.

Rollo May in *Power and Innocence* wrote that the May 4th killings and maimings at Kent marked an end in American of the concept of the innocent bystander. May 4th marked an end to many beliefs.

When ancient people were faced with an event

which puzzled, horrified and/or deeply hurt them, they sometimes concocted a story to help explain the happening to themselves. In that tradition, here is a story for you.

The North American continent, known by native Americans to be precious; described by early explorers to be wondrous; was beginning to lose heart. In fact, the earth was frightened for its very survival. Sometimes the planet felt it was nothing more than a giant garbage dump—a receptacle for waste generated by individuals and industry.

People were beginning to lose their nobility. They were frightened and afraid. They were forgetting that they were part of the earth and that the earth was a part of them.

Some people were becoming mean. They were separating themselves from the center. Those who were most frail, those who had the least, were blamed the most. They continued to silence the youth of the planet.

"Hating others" had become fashionable and mouthing of that hate was considered entertainment. Truth was considered unsophisticated and lies governed much of life. People gathered in great numbers to feign their amazement at the emperor's new clothes and to congratulate him on his choice of tailors.

Compassion was equated with weakness. People were neglecting to listen to their hearts. Justice was for sale. Courage had become associated with weapons.

118

Reverence for lives of people and for the elements of the universe was considered folly. People had forgotten that all men are created equal, endowed by their creator with certain inalienable rights—that among those are life . . . .

People had disconnected themselves from the land.

Many great teachings had been cast aside.

The young no longer had help understanding the unknown, the exotic, or the different. The earth had become a land of laws, which were applicable only to some.

The planet, our mother, was sad and fearful and She called together our sisters—as Chief Seattle called them, the flowers.

The planet told of her concern and suggested it was time to remind the people of the earth and the elements of the earth that they are part of the Great Universe. That what is done to one is done to all.

The earth asked the flowers to find those who needed solace and to comfort them. To find those who had lost their connection to the source and to remind them that the earth, its peoples, its plants, its animals, its birds, its tiny insects, its beauty and its truths are one.

And so that spring our sisters, the fragrant and beautiful flowers helped by our brothers, the rivers, came to the mountains in numbers never before recorded.

The colors were magnificent: deep, golden orange, white, red, pink, brilliant yellow and the sixteen shades of blues and purples. And people were truly amazed.

And they were filled with wonder. And they thanked the earth for giving them flowers.

THE END

Recommended Readings

Davies, Peter, & Board of Church and Society of the United Methodist Church. *The Truth About Kent State: A Challenge to the American Conscience.* Farrar Straus, New York, 1973.

Kisseloff, Jeff, *Voices of Protest From the 1960s: An Oral History,* The University Press of Kentucky, Lexington, 2007.

Stone, I.F., *The Killings at Kent State: How Murder Went Unpunished,* A New York Review Book, New York, 1973.

Kent and Jackson State 1970-1990: A Special Issue of Vietnam Generation. Volume 2, Number 2, Silver Spring, Maryland, 1990.

KENT STATE TRUTH TRIBUNAL. 2010
www.truthtribunal.org

Acknowledgements

As time has passed, many people have helped me with this manuscript whether I happened to be actively working on it or not. Those I wish to recognize in alphabetical order include:

Marna Seltabol Akerley
Hildie Becker
Deb Brunson
Esther Buchanan Bohuslov
Leigh Garrison
Tom Grace
Bonnie Henry
Hidden River Ranch
Laurel Krause
Barry Levine
Linda Lynch
Timothy J. McAndrews
Michael Moore
Jim Murphy
My Students
Helena Day Myers
Annie McCullough Richardson
Lorna Wilkes Ruebelmann
Paula Travis
Bette Waters

About The Author

Barbara Agte has worked as a high school English teacher (Eagle Pass, Texas) a college English Instructor (University of Wyoming, Kent State University, Western New Mexico University) a social worker (Natrona County Department of Social Services, The Dialysis Clinic, Deming Public Schools) and a costume constructionist and designer for Casper Costume, Casper College, Santa Fe Opera, New Mexico State University, Tumbleweed Theatre (Columbus N.M.) Creede Repertory Theatre (Creede, Colorado), Sculpture Basis, (Santa Fe, N.M.), Silver City (N.M.) Repertory Theatre.

Her writings have been published in DESERT EXPOSURE, and DESERT WINDS MAGAZINE.

She has a M.A. (Sul Ross University) and a M.S.S.A. (Case Western Reserve University), and she completed four years of doctoral work at Kent State University.

Cover photo of author by Timothy James McAndrews.

CPSIA information can be obtained at www.ICGtesting.com
Printed in the USA
BVOW030809110512

289939BV00001B/22/P